M000187955

GIVEN TO:

_____

GIVEN BY:

_____

DATE:

_____

Freeman-Smith, a division of Worthy Media, Inc.
134 Franklin Road, Suite 200, Brentwood, Tennessee 37027

*The quoted ideas expressed in this book (but not Scripture verses) are not, in all cases, exact quota-
tions, as some have been edited for clarity and brevity. In all cases, the author has attempted to
maintain the speaker's original intent. In some cases, quoted material for this book was obtained from
secondary sources, primarily print media. While every effort was made to ensure the accuracy of these
sources, the accuracy cannot be guaranteed. For additions, deletions, corrections, or clarifications in
future editions of this text, please write Freeman-Smith.*

Scripture quotations are taken from:

The Holy Bible, King James Version (KJV)

The Holy Bible, New International Version (NIV) Copyright © 1973, 1978, 1984, by
International Bible Society. Used by permission of Zondervan Publishing House. All rights
reserved.

The Holy Bible, New King James Version (NKJV) Copyright © 1982 by Thomas Nelson,
Inc. Used by permission.

The Holman Christian Standard Bible™ (HCSB) Copyright © 1999, 2000, 2001 by Holman
Bible Publishers. Used by permission.

Cover Design by Kim Russell / Wahoo Designs
Page Layout by Bart Dawson

ISBN 978-1-60587-334-3

Printed in the United States of America

30 PROMISES AND PRAYERS

OF

COURAGE

FOR MEN

TABLE OF CONTENTS

INTRODUCTION

God's promises are eternal and unchanging. But, as every man knows, life in today's fast-paced world can be so demanding and so confusing that it becomes easy to forget God's blessings and His mercy. This book invites you to slow down and remind yourself of the joys and abundance that God offers to all His children, including you.

How desperately our world needs Christian men who are willing to honor God with their service. This generation faces problems that defy easy solutions, yet face them we must. We need leaders whose vision is clear and whose intentions are pure. Daniel writes, "Those who are wise will shine like the brightness of the heavens, and those who lead many to righteousness, like the stars for ever and ever" (12:3 NIV). Hopefully, you are determined to be such a man—a courageous man who offers counsel and direction to his family, to his friends, and to his coworkers.

In your hands, you hold a book that contains 30 devotional readings. Each chapter contains Bible verses, a brief essay, inspirational quotations, and a prayer for your journey. During the next 30 days, please try this experiment: read a chapter each day. If you're already committed to a daily time of worship, this book will enrich that experience. If you are not, the simple act of giving God a few minutes each morning will change the direction and the quality of your life.

CHAPTER 1

LIVING COURAGEOUSLY

The Lord is the One who will go before you.
He will be with you;
He will not leave you or forsake you.
Do not be afraid or discouraged.

—

DEUTERONOMY 31:8 HCSB

Christians have every reason to live courageously. After all, the ultimate battle has already been fought and won on the cross at Calvary. But, even dedicated followers of Christ may find their courage tested by the inevitable disappointments and tragedies that occur in the lives of believers and non-believers alike.

Every human life is a tapestry of events: some wonderful, some not-so-wonderful, and some downright disheartening. When the storm clouds form overhead and we find ourselves wandering through the dark valley of despair, our faith is stretched, sometimes to the breaking point. But as believers, we can be comforted: Wherever we find ourselves, whether at the top of the mountain or the depths of the valley, God is there, and because He cares for us, we can live courageously.

The next time you find yourself in a fear-provoking situation, remember that God is as near as your next breath, and remember that He offers salvation to His children. He is your shield and your strength; He is your protector and your deliverer. Call upon Him in your hour of need and then be comforted. Whatever your challenge, whatever your trouble, God can handle it. And will.

MORE PROMISES FROM GOD'S WORD

Be alert, stand firm in the faith, be brave and strong.

1 Corinthians 16:13 HCSB

For God has not given us a spirit of fearfulness, but one of power, love, and sound judgment.

2 Timothy 1:7 HCSB

But when Jesus heard it, He answered him, "Don't be afraid. Only believe."

Luke 8:50 HCSB

So we may boldly say: "The Lord is my helper; I will not fear. What can man do to me?"

Hebrews 13:6 NKJV

11

MORE GREAT IDEAS

There comes a time when we simply have to face the challenges in our lives and stop backing down.

John Eldredge

Down through the centuries, in times of trouble and trial, God has brought courage to the hearts of those who love Him. The Bible is filled with assurances of God's help and comfort in every kind of trouble which might cause fears to arise in the human heart. You can look ahead with promise, hope, and joy.

Billy Graham

Jesus Christ can make the weakest man into a divine dreadnought, fearing nothing.

Oswald Chambers

Take courage. We walk in the wilderness today and in the Promised Land tomorrow.

D. L. Moody

Faith not only can help you through a crisis, it can help you to approach life after the hard times with a whole new perspective. It can help you adopt an outlook of hope and courage through faith to face reality.

John Maxwell

Why rely on yourself and fall? Cast yourself upon His arm. Be not afraid. He will not let you slip. Cast yourself in confidence. He will receive you and heal you.

St. Augustine

A PRAYER FOR TODAY

Dear Lord, fill me with Your Spirit and help me face my challenges with courage and determination. Keep me mindful, Father, that You are with me always—and with You by my side, I have nothing to fear. Amen

CHAPTER 2

THE POWER OF PRAYER

*The intense prayer of the righteous
is very powerful.*

—

JAMES 5:16 HCSB

"The power of prayer": these words are so familiar, yet sometimes we forget what they mean. Prayer is a powerful tool for communicating with our Creator; it is an opportunity to commune with the Giver of all things good. Prayer is not a thing to be taken lightly or to be used infrequently.

All too often, amid the rush of daily life, we may lose sight of God's presence in our lives. Instead of turning to Him for guidance and for comfort, we depend, instead, upon our own resources. To do so is a profound mistake. Prayer should never be reserved for mealtimes or for bedtimes; it should be an ever-present focus in our daily lives.

In his first letter to the Thessalonians, Paul wrote, "Rejoice evermore. Pray without ceasing. In every thing give thanks: for this is the will of God in Christ Jesus concerning you" (5:17-18 KJV). Paul's words apply to every Christian of every generation.

Today, instead of turning things over in our minds, let us turn them over to God in prayer. Instead of worrying about our decisions, let's trust God to help us make them. Today, let us pray constantly about things great and small. God is listening, and He wants to hear from us. Now.

MORE PROMISES FROM GOD'S WORD

Let the words of my mouth and the meditation of my heart be acceptable in Your sight, O Lord, my strength and my Redeemer.

Psalm 19:14 NKJV

Yet He often withdrew to deserted places and prayed.

Luke 5:16 HCSB

Don't worry about anything, but in everything, through prayer and petition with thanksgiving, let your requests be made known to God.

Philippians 4:6 HCSB

The Lord is far from the wicked but he hears the prayer of the righteous.

Proverbs 15:29 NIV

MORE GREAT IDEAS

Obedience is the master key to effective prayer.

Billy Graham

Those who know God the best are the richest and most powerful in prayer. Little acquaintance with God, and strangeness and coldness to Him, make prayer a rare and feeble thing.

E. M. Bounds

Learn to pray to God in such a way that you are trusting Him as your Physician to do what He knows is best. Confess to Him the disease, and let Him choose the remedy.

St. Augustine

Pour out your heart to God and tell Him how you feel. Be real, be honest, and when you get it all out, you'll start to feel the gradual covering of God's comforting presence.

Bill Hybels

God delights in the prayers of His children—prayers that express our love for Him, prayers that share our deepest burdens with Him.

Billy Graham

Prayer may not get us what we want, but it will teach us to want what we need.

Vance Havner

A PRAYER FOR TODAY

Dear Lord, make me a man of constant prayer. Your Holy Word commands me to pray without ceasing. Let me take everything to You. When I am discouraged, let me pray. When I am lonely, let me take my sorrows to You. When I grieve, let me take my tears to You, Lord, in prayer. And when I am joyful, let me offer up prayers of thanksgiving. In all things great and small, at all times, whether happy or sad, let me seek Your wisdom and Your grace . . . in prayer. Amen

CHAPTER 3

TRUSTING GOD'S PROMISES

*All Scripture is inspired by God and is profitable
for teaching, for rebuking, for correcting,
for training in righteousness,
so that the man of God may be complete,
equipped for every good work.*

—

2 TIMOTHY 3:16-17 HCSB

God's promises are found in a book like no other: the Holy Bible. The Bible is a roadmap for life here on earth and for life eternal. As Christians, we are called upon to trust its promises, to follow its commandments, and to share its Good News.

As believers, we must study the Bible daily and meditate upon its meaning for our lives. Otherwise, we deprive ourselves of a priceless gift from our Creator. God's Holy Word is, indeed, a transforming, life-changing, one-of-a-kind treasure. And, a passing acquaintance with the Good Book is insufficient for Christians who seek to obey God's Word and to understand His will.

God has made promises to mankind and to you. God's promises never fail and they never grow old. You must trust those promises and share them with your family, with your friends, and with the world.

MORE PROMISES FROM GOD'S WORD

Man shall not live by bread alone, but by every word that proceeds from the mouth of God.

Matthew 4:4 NKJV

For I am not ashamed of the gospel, because it is God's power for salvation to everyone who believes.

Romans 1:16 HCSB

Heaven and earth will pass away, but My words will never pass away.

Matthew 24:35 HCSB

For the word of God is living and effective and sharper than any two-edged sword, penetrating as far as to divide soul, spirit, joints, and marrow; it is a judge of the ideas and thoughts of the heart.

Hebrews 4:12 HCSB

Your word is a lamp for my feet and a light on my path.

Psalm 119:105 HCSB

MORE GREAT IDEAS

Nobody ever outgrows Scripture; the book widens and deepens with our years.

C. H. Spurgeon

Faith is the virtue that enables us to believe and obey the Word of God, for faith comes from hearing and hearing from the Word of God.

Franklin Graham

Meditating upon His Word will inevitably bring peace of mind, strength of purpose, and power for living.

Bill Bright

When you meet with God, open the Bible. Don't rely on your memory; rely on those printed pages.

Charles Swindoll

It takes calm, thoughtful, prayerful meditation on the Word to extract its deepest nourishment.

Vance Havner

Cling to the whole Bible, not to part of it. A man is not going to do much with a broken sword.

D. L. Moody

My meditation and study have shown me that, like God, His Word is holy, everlasting, absolutely true, powerful, personally fair, and never changing.

Bill Bright

Words fail to express my love for this holy Book, my gratitude for its author, for His love and goodness. How shall I thank him for it?

Lottie Moon

A PRAYER FOR TODAY

Heavenly Father, Your Holy Word is a light unto the world; let me study it, trust it, and share it with all who cross my path. In all that I do, help me be a worthy witness for You as I share the Good News of Your perfect Son and Your perfect Word. Amen

CHAPTER 4

BEYOND WORRY

Don't worry about anything, but in everything,
through prayer and petition with thanksgiving,
let your requests be made known to God.
—

PHILIPPIANS 4:6 HCSB

If you are a man with lots of obligations and plenty of responsibilities, it is simply a fact of life: You worry. From time to time, you worry about health, about finances, about safety, about family, and about countless other concerns, some great and some small.

Where is the best place to take your worries? Take them to God. Take your troubles to Him; take your fears to Him; take your doubts to Him; take your weaknesses to Him; take your sorrows to Him . . . and leave them all there. Seek protection from the One who offers you eternal salvation; build your spiritual house upon the Rock that cannot be moved.

Perhaps you are uncertain about your future or your finances—or perhaps you are simply a "worrier" by nature. If so, it's time to focus less on your troubles and more on God's promises. And that's as it should be because God is trustworthy . . . and you are protected.

MORE PROMISES FROM GOD'S WORD

Your heart must not be troubled. Believe in God;
believe also in Me.

John 14:1 HCSB

Come to Me, all you who labor and are heavy
laden, and I will give you rest. Take My yoke upon
you and learn from Me, for I am gentle and lowly
in heart, and you will find rest for your souls. For
My yoke is easy and My burden is light.

Matthew 11:28-30 NKJV

I will be with you when you pass through the
waters . . . when you walk through the fire . . . the
flame will not burn you. For I the Lord your God,
the Holy One of Israel, and your Savior.

Isaiah 43:2-3 HCSB

Don't worry about your life, what you will eat or
what you will drink; or about your body, what you
will wear. Isn't life more than food and the body
more than clothing?

Matthew 6:25 HCSB

MORE GREAT IDEAS

God is bigger than your problems. Whatever worries press upon you today, put them in God's hands and leave them there.

Billy Graham

Today is the tomorrow we worried about yesterday.

Dennis Swanberg

The beginning of anxiety is the end of faith, and the beginning of true faith is the end of anxiety.

George Mueller

Pray, and let God worry.

Martin Luther

We know so little about the future that to worry about it would be the height of foolishness.

C. H. Spurgeon

Worry and anxiety are sand in the machinery of life; faith is the oil.

E. Stanley Jones

Much that worries us beforehand can, quite unexpectedly, have a happy and simple solution. Worries just don't matter. Things really are in a better hand than ours.

Dietrich Bonhoeffer

A PRAYER FOR TODAY

Forgive me, Lord, when I worry. Worry reflects a lack of trust in Your ability to meet my every need. Help me to work, Lord, and not to worry. And, keep me mindful, Father, that nothing, absolutely nothing, will happen this day that You and I cannot handle together. Amen

CHAPTER 5

THE RIGHT KIND OF LEADERSHIP

—◦◦◦—

According to the grace given to us, we have different gifts: If prophecy, use it according to the standard of faith; if service, in service; if teaching, in teaching; if exhorting, in exhortation; giving, with generosity; leading, with diligence; showing mercy, with cheerfulness.

—

ROMANS 12:6-8 HCSB

The old saying is familiar and true: imitation is the sincerest form of flattery. As believers, we are called to imitate, as best we can, the carpenter from Galilee. The task of imitating Christ is often difficult and sometimes impossible, but as Christians, we must continue to try.

Our world needs leaders who willingly honor Christ with their words and their deeds, but not necessarily in that order. If you seek to be such a leader, then you must begin by making yourself a worthy example to your family, to your friends, to your church, and to your community. After all, your words of instruction will never ring true unless you yourself are willing to follow them.

Christ-centered leadership is an exercise in service: service to God in heaven and service to His children here on earth. Christ willingly became a servant to His followers, and you must seek to do the same for yours.

Are you the kind of servant-leader whom you would want to follow? If so, congratulations: you are honoring your Savior by imitating Him. And that, of course, is the sincerest form of flattery.

MORE PROMISES FROM GOD'S WORD

And we exhort you, brothers: warn those who are lazy, comfort the discouraged, help the weak, be patient with everyone.

1 Thessalonians 5:14 HCSB

Shepherd God's flock among you, not overseeing out of compulsion but freely, according to God's will; not for the money but eagerly.

1 Peter 5:2 HCSB

An overseer, therefore, must be above reproach, the husband of one wife, self-controlled, sensible, respectable, hospitable, an able teacher, not addicted to wine, not a bully but gentle, not quarrelsome, not greedy.

1 Timothy 3:2-3 HCSB

His master said to him, "Well done, good and faithful slave! You were faithful over a few things; I will put you in charge of many things. Enter your master's joy!"

Matthew 25:21 HCSB

MORE GREAT IDEAS

A true and safe leader is likely to be one who has no desire to lead, but is forced into a position of leadership by inward pressure of the Holy Spirit and the press of external situation.

A. W. Tozer

A wise leader chooses a variety of gifted individuals. He complements his strengths.

Charles Stanley

You can never separate a leader's actions from his character.

John Maxwell

What do we Christians chiefly value in our leaders? The answer seems to be not their holiness, but their gifts and skills and resources. The thought that only holy people are likely to be spiritually useful does not loom large in our minds.

J. I. Packer

Leaders must learn how to wait. Often their followers don't always see as far as they see or have the faith that they have.

Warren Wiersbe

The test of a leader is taking the vision from me to we.

John Maxwell

Integrity and maturity are two character traits vital to the heart of a leader.

Charles Stanley

A PRAYER FOR TODAY

Dear Lord, when I find myself in a position of leadership, let me seek Your will and obey Your commandments. Make me a man of integrity and wisdom, Lord, and make me a worthy example to those whom I serve. Let me be a Christ-centered leader, and let me turn to You, Father, for guidance, for courage, for wisdom, and for love. Amen

CHAPTER 6

FINDING PURPOSE

I will instruct you and show you the way to go;
with My eye on you, I will give counsel.

—

PSALM 32:8 HCSB

God has a plan for your life—a plan that is near and dear to His heart. If you genuinely seek to fulfill God's plan for your life, then you must do this: you must make decisions that are pleasing to Him. The most important decision of your life is, of course, your commitment to accept God's Son as your personal Lord and Savior. And, once your eternal destiny is secured, you will undoubtedly ask yourself the question "What now, Lord?" If you earnestly seek God's will, you will find it . . . in time.

Life is best lived on purpose. And purpose, like everything else in the universe, begins in the heart of God. Whether you realize it or not, God has a direction for your life, a divine calling, a path along which He intends to lead you. When you welcome God into your heart and establish a genuine relationship with Him, He will begin—and He will continue—to make His purposes known.

Sometimes, God's intentions will be clear to you; other times, God's plan will seem uncertain at best. But even on those difficult days when you are unsure which way to turn, you must never lose sight of these overriding facts:

God created you for a reason; He has important work for you to do; and He's waiting patiently for you to do it. So why not begin today?

MORE PROMISES FROM GOD'S WORD

We know that all things work together for the good of those who love God: those who are called according to His purpose.

Romans 8:28 HCSB

For it is God who is working among you both the willing and the working for His good purpose.

Philippians 2:13 HCSB

You reveal the path of life to me; in Your presence is abundant joy; in Your right hand are eternal pleasures.

Psalm 16:11 HCSB

Commit your activities to the Lord and your plans will be achieved.

Proverbs 16:3 HCSB

MORE GREAT IDEAS

Without God, life has no purpose, and without purpose, life has no meaning.

Rick Warren

Continually restate to yourself what the purpose of your life is.

Oswald Chambers

Waiting means going about our assigned tasks, confident that God will provide the meaning and the conclusions.

Eugene Peterson

The worst thing that laziness does is rob a man of spiritual purpose.

Billy Graham

Whatever purpose motivates your life, it must be something big enough and grand enough to make the investment worthwhile.

Warren Wiersbe

Their distress is due entirely to their deliberate determination to use themselves for a purpose other than God's.

Oswald Chambers

When God speaks to you through the Bible, prayer, circumstances, the church, or in some other way, he has a purpose in mind for your life.

Henry Blackaby and Claude King

A PRAYER FOR TODAY

Dear Lord, I know that You have a purpose for my life, and I will seek that purpose today and every day that I live. Let my actions be pleasing to You, and let me share Your Good News with a world that so desperately needs Your healing hand and the salvation of Your Son. Amen

CHAPTER 7

WORKING FOR
THE LORD

Whatever you do, do it enthusiastically,
as something done for the Lord
and not for men.

—

COLOSSIANS 3:23 HCSB

The old adage is both familiar and true: We must pray as if everything depended upon God, but work as if everything depended upon us. Yet sometimes, when we are weary and discouraged, we may allow our worries to sap our energy and our hope. God has other intentions. God intends that we pray for things, and He intends that we be willing to work for the things that we pray for. More importantly, God intends that our work should become His work.

Are you willing to work diligently for yourself, for your family, and for your God? And are you willing to engage in work that is pleasing to your Creator? If so, you can expect your Heavenly Father to bring forth a rich harvest.

And if you have concerns about the inevitable challenges of everyday living, take those concerns to God in prayer. He will guide your steps, He will steady your hand, He will calm your fears, and He will reward your efforts.

MORE PROMISES FROM GOD'S WORD

He did it with all his heart. So he prospered.

2 Chronicles 31:21 NKJV

Whatever your hands find to do, do with [all] your strength.

Ecclesiastes 9:10 HCSB

Don't work only while being watched, in order to please men, but as slaves of Christ, do God's will from your heart. Render service with a good attitude, as to the Lord and not to men.

Ephesians 6:6-7 HCSB

We must do the works of Him who sent Me while it is day. Night is coming when no one can work.

John 9:4 HCSB

The people had a mind to work.

Nehemiah 4:6 KJV

41

MORE GREAT IDEAS

Thank God every morning when you get up that you have something which must be done, whether you like it or not. Work breeds a hundred virtues that idleness never knows.

Charles Kingsley

It may be that the day of judgment will dawn tomorrow; in that case, we shall gladly stop working for a better tomorrow. But not before.

Dietrich Bonhoeffer

We must trust as if it all depended on God and work as if it all depended on us.

C. H. Spurgeon

When we wholeheartedly commit ourselves to God, there is nothing mediocre or run-of-the-mill about us. To live for Christ is to be passionate about our Lord and about our lives.

Jim Gallery

The world does not consider labor a blessing, therefore it flees and hates it, but the pious who fear the Lord labor with a ready and cheerful heart, for they know God's command, and they acknowledge His calling.

Martin Luther

Few things fire up a person's commitment like dedication to excellence.

John Maxwell

Freedom is not an absence of responsibility; but rather a reward we receive when we've performed our responsibility with excellence.

Charles Swindoll

A PRAYER FOR TODAY

Dear Lord, make my work pleasing to You. Help me to sow the seeds of Your abundance everywhere I go. Let me be diligent in all my undertakings and give me patience to wait for Your harvest. Amen

CHAPTER 8

LIVING HUMBLY

—◆—

Do nothing out of rivalry or conceit,
but in humility consider others as
more important than yourselves.

—

PHILIPPIANS 2:3 HCSB

As fallible human beings, we have so much to humble about. Why, then, is humility such a difficult trait for us to master? Precisely because we are fallible human beings. Yet, if we are to grow and mature as Christians, we must strive to give credit where credit is due, starting, of course, with God and His only begotten Son.

As Christians, we have been refashioned and saved by Jesus Christ, and that salvation came not because of our own good works but because of God's grace. Thus, we are not "self-made"; we are "God-made" and we are "Christ-saved." How, then, can we be boastful? The answer, of course, is that, if we are honest with ourselves and with our God, we simply can't be boastful . . . we must, instead, be eternally grateful and exceedingly humble. Humility, however, is not easy for most of us. All too often, we are tempted to stick out our chests and say, "Look at me; look what I did!" But, in the quiet moments when we search the depths of our own hearts, we know better. Whatever "it" is, God did that. And He deserves the credit.

MORE PROMISES FROM GOD'S WORD

Humble yourselves therefore under the mighty hand of God, so that He may exalt you in due time, casting all your care upon Him, because He cares about you.

1 Peter 5:6-7 HCSB

You will save the humble people; But Your eyes are on the haughty, that You may bring them down.

2 Samuel 22:28 NKJV

If My people who are called by My name will humble themselves, and pray and seek My face, and turn from their wicked ways, then I will hear from heaven, and will forgive their sin and heal their land.

2 Chronicles 7:14 NKJV

Humble yourselves before the Lord, and He will exalt you.

James 4:10 HCSB

MORE GREAT IDEAS

Jesus had a humble heart. If He abides in us, pride will never dominate our lives.

Billy Graham

Humility is the fairest and rarest flower that blooms.

Charles Swindoll

We can never have more of true faith than we have of true humility.

Andrew Murray

Let the love of Christ be believed in and felt in your hearts, and it will humble you.

C. H. Spurgeon

Humility is an attitude. The Lord is high and lifted up, and we are supposed to take a position of lowliness.

Franklin Graham

A humble heart is like a magnet that draws the favor of God toward us.

Jim Cymbala

Because Christ Jesus came to the world clothed in humility, he will always be found among those who are clothed with humility. He will be found among the humble people.

A. W. Tozer

A PRAYER FOR TODAY

Lord, make me a man with a humble heart. Keep me mindful, Dear God, that all my gifts come from You. When I feel prideful, remind me that You sent Your Son to be a humble carpenter and that Jesus was ridiculed on a cross. Let me grow beyond my need for earthly praise, Lord, and when I seek approval, let me look only to You. Amen

CHAPTER 9

THE IMPORTANCE OF CHARACTER

As in water face reflects face,
so a man's heart reveals the man.

PROVERBS 27:19 NKJV

Charles Swindoll correctly observed, "Nothing speaks louder or more powerfully than a life of integrity." Righteous men agree.

Character is built slowly over a lifetime. It is the sum of every right decision, every honest word, every noble thought, and every heartfelt prayer. It is forged on the anvil of honorable work and polished by the twin virtues of generosity and humility. Character is a precious thing—difficult to build but easy to tear down. As believers in Christ, we must seek to live each day with discipline, honesty, and faith. When we do, integrity becomes a habit.

If you sincerely wish to be a righteous man, then you must walk with God and you must follow His commandments. When you do, your character will take care of itself . . . and God will surely smile upon you and yours.

MORE PROMISES FROM GOD'S WORD

As the water reflects the face, so the heart reflects the person.

Proverbs 27:19 HCSB

Do not be deceived: "Evil company corrupts good habits."

1 Corinthians 15:33 NKJV

We also rejoice in our afflictions, because we know that affliction produces endurance, endurance produces proven character, and proven character produces hope.

Romans 5:3-4 HCSB

Now don't be afraid, my daughter. I will do for you whatever you say, since all the people in my town know that you are a woman of noble character.

Ruth 3:11 HCSB

A good name is to be chosen rather than great riches, loving favor rather than silver and gold.

Proverbs 22:1 NKJV

MORE GREAT IDEAS

The trials of life can be God's tools for engraving His image on our character.

Warren Wiersbe

There is no way to grow a saint overnight. Character, like the oak tree, does not spring up like a mushroom.

Vance Havner

Character is both developed and revealed by tests, and all of life is a test.

Rick Warren

Character is made in the small moments of our lives.

Phillips Brooks

Integrity is not a given factor in everyone's life. It is a result of self-discipline, inner trust, and a decision to be relentlessly honest in all situations in our lives.

John Maxwell

Honesty has a beautiful and refreshing simplicity about it. No ulterior motives. No hidden meanings. As honesty and integrity characterize our lives, there will be no need to manipulate others.

Charles Swindoll

Integrity is the glue that holds our way of life together. We must constantly strive to keep our integrity intact. When wealth is lost, nothing is lost; when health is lost, something is lost; when character is lost, all is lost.

Billy Graham

A PRAYER FOR TODAY

Dear Lord, make me a man whose conduct is honorable. Make me a man whose words are true. Give me the wisdom to know right from wrong, and give me the courage—and the skill—to do what needs to be done in the service of Your Son. Amen

CHAPTER 10

THE POWER OF ENCOURAGEMENT

Anxiety in a man's heart weighs it down,
but a good word cheers it up.

—

PROVERBS 12:25 HCSB

Life is a team sport, and all of us need occasional pats on the back from our teammates. As Christians, we are called upon to spread the Good News of Christ, and we are also called to spread a message of encouragement and hope to the world.

In the book of Ephesians, Paul writes, "Do not let any unwholesome talk come out of your mouths, but only what is helpful for building others up according to their needs, that it may benefit those who listen" (4:29 NIV). Paul reminds us that when we choose our words carefully, we can have a powerful impact on those around us.

Whether you realize it or not, many people with whom you come in contact every day are in desperate need of a smile or an encouraging word. The world can be a difficult place, and countless friends and family members may be troubled by the challenges of everyday life. Since we don't always know who needs our help, the best strategy is to encourage all the people who cross our paths. So today, be a world-class source of encouragement to everyone you meet. Never has the need been greater.

MORE PROMISES FROM GOD'S WORD

Carry one another's burdens; in this way you will fulfill the law of Christ.

Galatians 6:2 HCSB

I want their hearts to be encouraged and joined together in love, so that they may have all the riches of assured understanding, and have the knowledge of God's mystery—Christ.

Colossians 2:2 HCSB

But encourage each other daily, while it is still called today, so that none of you is hardened by sin's deception.

Hebrews 3:13 HCSB

And let us be concerned about one another in order to promote love and good works.

Hebrews 10:24 HCSB

Therefore encourage one another and build each other up as you are already doing.

1 Thessalonians 5:11 HCSB

MORE GREAT IDEAS

A lot of people have gone further than they thought they could because someone else thought they could.

Zig Ziglar

God grant that we may not hinder those who are battling their way slowly into the light.

Oswald Chambers

We have the Lord, but He Himself has recognized that we need the touch of a human hand. He Himself came down and lived among us as a man. We cannot see Him now, but blessed be the tie that binds human hearts in Christian love.

Vance Havner

I can usually sense that a leading is from the Holy Spirit when it calls me to humble myself, to serve somebody, to encourage somebody, or to give something away. Very rarely will the evil one lead us to do those kind of things.

Bill Hybels

The truest help we can render an afflicted man is not to take his burden from him, but to call out his best energy, that he may be able to bear the burden himself.

Phillips Brooks

It is helpful to remember the distinction between appreciation and affirmation. We appreciate what a person does, but we affirm who a person is.

Charles Swindoll

A PRAYER FOR TODAY

Dear Lord, let me celebrate the accomplishments of others. Make me a source of genuine, lasting encouragement to my family and friends. And let my words and deeds be worthy of Your Son, the One who gives me strength and salvation, this day and for all eternity. Amen

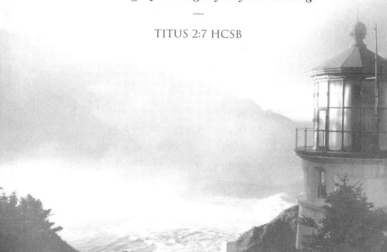

CHAPTER 11

THE RIGHT KIND OF EXAMPLE

*Set an example of good works yourself,
with integrity and dignity in your teaching.*

—

TITUS 2:7 HCSB

Okay, here's a question: What kind of example are you? Are you the kind of man whose life serves as a powerful example of decency and morality? Are you a man whose behavior serves as a positive role model for others? Are you the kind of man whose actions, day in and day out, are based upon integrity, fidelity, and a love for the Lord? If so, you are not only blessed by God, but you are also a powerful force for good in a world that desperately needs positive influences such as yours.

We live in a dangerous, temptation-filled world. That's why you encounter so many opportunities to stray from God's commandments. Resist those temptations! When you do, you'll earn God's blessings and you'll serve as a positive role model for your family and friends.

Phillips Brooks advised, "Be such a man, and live such a life, that if every man were such as you, and every life a life like yours, this earth would be God's Paradise." And that's sound advice because our families and friends are watching . . . and so, for that matter, is God.

MORE PROMISES FROM GOD'S WORD

Therefore since we also have such a large cloud of witnesses surrounding us, let us lay aside every weight and the sin that so easily ensnares us, and run with endurance the race that lies before us.

Hebrews 12:1 HCSB

For the kingdom of God is not in talk but in power.

1 Corinthians 4:20 HCSB

You should be an example to the believers in speech, in conduct, in love, in faith, in purity.

1 Timothy 4:12 HCSB

Do everything without grumbling and arguing, so that you may be blameless and pure.

Philippians 2:14–15 HCSB

For you were once darkness, but now you are light in the Lord. Walk as children of light—for the fruit of the light results in all goodness, righteousness, and truth—discerning what is pleasing to the Lord.

Ephesians 5:8-10 HCSB

MORE GREAT IDEAS

Having a doctrine pass before the mind is not what the Bible means by knowing the truth. It's only when it reaches down deep into the heart that the truth begins to set us free, just as a key must penetrate a lock to turn it, or as rainfall must saturate the earth down to the roots in order for your garden to grow.

John Eldredge

There is no way to grow a saint overnight. Character, like the oak tree, does not spring up like a mushroom.

Vance Havner

If we have the true love of God in our hearts, we will show it in our lives. We will not have to go up and down the earth proclaiming it. We will show it in everything we say or do.

D. L. Moody

Integrity of heart is indispensable.

John Calvin

What we practice, not (save at rare intervals) what we preach, is usually our great contribution to the conversion of others.

C. S. Lewis

The sermon of your life in tough times ministers to people more powerfully than the most eloquent speaker.

Bill Bright

The best evidence of our having the truth is our walking in the truth.

Matthew Henry

A PRAYER FOR TODAY

Dear Lord, let my light shine brightly for You. Let me be a positive example for all to see, and let me share love and kindness with my family and friends, today and every day. Amen

CHAPTER 12

USING YOUR TALENTS

Do not neglect the gift that is in you.

—

1 TIMOTHY 4:14 HCSB

God knew precisely what He was doing when He gave you a unique set of talents and opportunities. And now, God wants you to use those talents for the glory of His kingdom. So here's the $64,000 question: are you going to use those talents, or not?

Our Heavenly Father instructs us to be faithful stewards of the gifts that He bestows upon us. But we live in a world that encourages us to do otherwise. Ours is a society that is filled to the brim with countless opportunities to squander our time, our resources, and our talents. So we must be watchful for distractions and temptations that might lead us astray.

If you're sincerely interested in building a successful career, build it upon the talents that God (in His infinite wisdom) has given you. Don't try to build a career around the talents you wish He had given you.

God has blessed you with unique opportunities to serve Him, and He has given you every tool that you need to do so. Today, accept this challenge: value the talent that God has given you, nourish it, make it grow, and share it with the world. After all, the best way to say "Thank You" for God's gifts is to use them.

MORE PROMISES FROM GOD'S WORD

So he who had received five talents came and brought five other talents, saying, "Lord, you delivered to me five talents; look, I have gained five more talents besides them." His lord said to him, "Well done, good and faithful servant; you were faithful over a few things, I will make you ruler over many things. Enter into the joy of your lord."

Matthew 25:20-21 NKJV

Each one has his own gift from God, one in this manner and another in that.

1 Corinthians 7:7 NKJV

I remind you to keep ablaze the gift of God that is in you.

2 Timothy 1:6 HCSB

Based on the gift they have received, everyone should use it to serve others, as good managers of the varied grace of God.

1 Peter 4:10 HCSB

MORE GREAT IDEAS

You are a unique blend of talents, skills, and gifts, which makes you an indispensable member of the body of Christ.

Charles Stanley

God has given you a unique set of talents and opportunities—talents and opportunities that can be built up or buried—and the choice to build or bury is entirely up to you.

Jim Gallery

Employ whatever God has entrusted you with, in doing good, all possible good, in every possible kind and degree.

John Wesley

In the great orchestra we call life, you have an instrument and a song, and you owe it to God to play them both sublimely.

Max Lucado

If you want to reach your potential, you need to add a strong work ethic to your talent.

John Maxwell

God often reveals His direction for our lives through the way He made us . . . with a certain personality and unique skills.

Bill Hybels

You are the only person on earth who can use your ability.

Zig Ziglar

A PRAYER FOR TODAY

Father, because of Your promises I can live courageously. But make me fearful of displeasing You. Let me fear complacency in doing Your kingdom's work, and make me a faithful steward of the gifts You have entrusted to me. Amen

CHAPTER 13

THE RULE THAT'S GOLDEN

*Just as you want others to do for you,
do the same for them.*

—

LUKE 6:31 HCSB

Is the Golden Rule your rule, or is it just another Bible verse that goes in one ear and out the other? Jesus made Himself perfectly clear: He instructed you to treat other people in the same way that you want to be treated. But sometimes, especially when you're feeling pressure from friends, or when you're tired or upset, obeying the Golden Rule can seem like an impossible task—but it's not.

God wants each of us to treat other people with respect, kindness, and courtesy. He wants us to rise above our own imperfections, and He wants us to treat others with unselfishness and love. To make it short and sweet, God wants us to obey the Golden Rule, and He knows we can do it.

So if you're wondering how to treat someone else, ask the person you see every time you look into the mirror. The answer you receive will tell you exactly what to do.

MORE PROMISES FROM GOD'S WORD

Therefore, whatever you want others to do for you, do also the same for them—this is the Law and the Prophets.

Matthew 7:12 HCSB

If you really carry out the royal law prescribed in Scripture, You shall love your neighbor as yourself, you are doing well.

James 2:8 HCSB

And let us not grow weary while doing good, for in due season we shall reap if we do not lose heart.

Galatians 6:9 NKJV

Be kindly affectionate to one another with brotherly love, in honor giving preference to one another; not lagging in diligence, fervent in spirit, serving the Lord; rejoicing in hope, patient in tribulation, continuing steadfastly in prayer.

Romans 12:10-12 NKJV

MORE GREAT IDEAS

Faith never asks whether good works are to be done, but has done them before there is time to ask the question, and it is always doing them.

Martin Luther

The #1 rule of friendship is the Golden one.

Jim Gallery

Do all the good you can. By all the means you can. In all the ways you can. In all the places you can. At all the times you can. To all the people you can. As long as ever you can.

John Wesley

We are never more like God than when we give.

Charles Swindoll

Abundant living means abundant giving.

E. Stanley Jones

The Golden Rule starts at home, but it should never stop there.

Marie T. Freeman

Our lives, we are told, are but fleeting at best, / Like roses they fade and decay; / Then let us do good while the present is ours, / Be useful as long as we stay.

Fanny Crosby

If you want to be truly happy, you won't find it on an endless quest for more stuff. You'll find it in receiving God's generosity and in passing that generosity along.

Bill Hybels

A PRAYER FOR TODAY

Dear God, help me remember to treat other people in the same way that I would want to be treated if I were in their shoes. The Golden Rule is Your rule, Father; I'll make it my rule, too. Amen

CHAPTER 14

OVERCOMING ADVERSITY

*Dear friends, when the fiery ordeal arises among
you to test you, don't be surprised by it,
as if something unusual were happening to you.
Instead, as you share in the sufferings
of the Messiah rejoice, so that you
may also rejoice with great joy at
the revelation of His glory.*

—

1 PETER 4:12-13 HCSB

From time to time, all of us face adversity, hardship, disappointment, and loss. Old Man Trouble pays periodic visits to each of us; none of us are exempt. When we are troubled, God stands ready and willing to protect us. Our responsibility, of course, is to ask Him for protection. When we call upon Him in heartfelt prayer, He will answer—in His own time and in accordance with His own perfect plan.

Our world continues to change, but God's love remains constant. And, He remains ready to comfort us and strengthen us whenever we turn to Him. Psalm 145 promises, "The Lord is near to all who call on him, to all who call on him in truth. He fulfills the desires of those who fear him; he hears their cry and saves them" (vv. 18-20 NIV).

Life is often challenging, but as Christians, we must not be afraid. God loves us, and He will protect us. In times of hardship, He will comfort us; in times of sorrow, He will dry our tears. When we are troubled, or weak, or sorrowful, God is always with us. We must build our lives on the rock that cannot be shaken . . . we must trust in God. Always.

MORE PROMISES FROM GOD'S WORD

I will be with you when you pass through the waters . . . when you walk through the fire . . . the flame will not burn you. For I the Lord your God, the Holy One of Israel, and your Savior.

Isaiah 43:2-3 HCSB

I called to the Lord in my distress; I called to my God. From His temple He heard my voice.

2 Samuel 22:7 HCSB

Consider it a great joy, my brothers, whenever you experience various trials, knowing that the testing of your faith produces endurance. But endurance must do its complete work, so that you may be mature and complete, lacking nothing.

James 1:2-4 HCSB

Whatever has been born of God conquers the world. This is the victory that has conquered the world: our faith.

1 John 5:4 HCSB

MORE GREAT IDEAS

God whispers to us in our pleasures, speaks in our conscience, but shouts in our pain.

C. S. Lewis

Life will be made or broken at the place where we meet and deal with obstacles.

E. Stanley Jones

As sure as God puts his children in the furnace, he will be in the furnace with them.

C. H. Spurgeon

Throughout history, when God's people found themselves facing impossible odds, they reminded themselves of God's limitless power.

Bill Hybels

The sermon of your life in tough times ministers to people more powerfully than the most eloquent speaker.

Bill Bright

The only way to learn a strong faith is to endure great trials. I have learned my faith by standing firm amid the most severe of tests.

George Mueller

If you learn to trust God with a child-like dependence on Him as your loving heavenly Father, no trouble can destroy you.

Billy Graham

A PRAYER FOR TODAY

Dear Heavenly Father, You are my strength and my protector. When I am troubled, You comfort me. When I am discouraged, You lift me up. When I am afraid, You deliver me. Let me turn to You, Lord, when I am weak. In times of adversity, let me trust Your plan and Your will for my life. Your love is infinite, as is Your wisdom. Whatever my circumstances, Dear Lord, let me always give the praise, and the thanks, and the glory to You. Amen

CHAPTER 15

TRUSTING GOD'S WILL

He is the Lord.
He will do what He thinks is good.

—

1 SAMUEL 3:18 HCSB

When Jesus confronted the reality of His impending death on the cross, He asked God that this terrible burden might be lifted. But as He faced the possibility of a suffering that was beyond description, Jesus prayed, "Nevertheless not my will, but thine, be done" (Luke 22:42 KJV). As Christians, we too must be willing to accept God's will, even when we do not fully understand the reasons for the hardships that we must endure.

Grief and suffering visit all of us who live long and love deeply. When we lose a loved one, or when we experience any other profound loss, darkness overwhelms us for a while, and it seems as if we cannot summon the strength to face another day—but, with God's help, we can. When we confront circumstances that trouble us to the very core of our souls, we must trust God. When we are worried, we must turn our concerns over to Him. When we are anxious, we must be still and listen for the quiet assurance of God's promises. And then, by placing our lives in His hands, we learn that He is our Shepherd today and throughout eternity. Let us trust the Shepherd.

MORE PROMISES FROM GOD'S WORD

Whoever does the will of God is My brother and sister and mother.

Mark 3:35 HCSB

Commit your activities to the Lord and your plans will be achieved.

Proverbs 16:3 HCSB

Father, if You are willing, take this cup away from Me—nevertheless, not My will, but Yours, be done.

Luke 22:42 HCSB

And do not be conformed to this world, but be transformed by the renewing of your mind, that you may prove what is that good and acceptable and perfect will of God.

Romans 12:2 NKJV

MORE GREAT IDEAS

Our Lord never asks us to decide for Him; He asks us to yield to Him—a very different matter.

Oswald Chambers

Absolute submission is not enough; we should go on to joyful acquiescence to the will of God.

C. H. Spurgeon

Our sense of joy, satisfaction, and fulfillment in life increases, no matter what the circumstances, if we are in the center of God's will.

Billy Graham

To walk out of His will is to walk into nowhere.

C. S. Lewis

A Christian seeking God's will must be certain that he has first relinquished control of his life, including his finances, and is truly seeking God's direction.

Larry Burkett

You cannot stay where you are and go with God. You cannot continue doing things your way and accomplish God's purposes in His ways. Your thinking cannot come close to God's thoughts. For you to do the will of God, you must adjust your life to Him, His purposes, and His ways.

Henry Blackaby

God does not furnish us with a detailed road map. When we are with Him, we may not always know whither, but we know with whom.

Vance Havner

A PRAYER FOR TODAY

Heavenly Father, in these quiet moments before this busy day unfolds, I come to You. I will study Your Word and seek Your guidance. Give me the wisdom to know Your will for my life and the courage to follow wherever You may lead me, today and forever. Amen

CHAPTER 16

AND THE GREATEST
OF THESE . . .

—◦◦◦—

Now these three remain: faith, hope, and love.
But the greatest of these is love.

—

1 CORINTHIANS 13:13 HCSB

Christ's words left no room for interpretation: "'Love the Lord your God with all your heart and with all your soul and with all your mind.' This is the first and greatest commandment. And the second is like it: 'Love your neighbor as yourself.' All the Law and the Prophets hang on these two commandments" (Matthew 22:37-40 NIV). But sometimes, despite our best intentions, we fall short. When we become embittered with ourselves, with our neighbors, or most especially with God, we disobey the One who gave His life for us.

If we are to please God, we must cleanse ourselves of the negative feelings that separate us from others and from Him. In 1 Corinthians 13, we are told that love is the foundation upon which all our relationships are to be built: our relationships with others and our relationship with our Maker. May we fill our hearts with love; may we never yield to bitterness. And may we praise the Son of God who, in His infinite wisdom, made love His greatest commandment.

MORE PROMISES FROM GOD'S WORD

If I speak the languages of men and of angels, but do not have love, I am a sounding gong or a clanging cymbal.

1 Corinthians 13:1 HCSB

I pray that you, being rooted and firmly established in love, may be able to comprehend with all the saints what is the breadth and width, height and depth, and to know the Messiah's love that surpasses knowledge, so you may be filled with all the fullness of God.

Ephesians 3:17-19 HCSB

We love because He first loved us.

1 John 4:19 HCSB

Dear friends, if God loved us in this way, we also must love one another.

1 John 4:11 HCSB

Mighty waters cannot extinguish love; rivers cannot sweep it away.

Song of Solomon 8:7 HCSB

MORE GREAT IDEAS

Truth becomes hard if it is not softened by love, and love becomes soft if not strengthened by truth.

E. Stanley Jones

Brotherly love is still the distinguishing badge of every true Christian.

Matthew Henry

Love must be supported and fed and protected, just like a little infant who is growing up at home.

James Dobson

Beware that you are not swallowed up in books! An ounce of love is worth a pound of knowledge.

John Wesley

The truth of the Gospel is intended to free us to love God and others with our whole heart.

John Eldredge

Forgiveness is the final form of love.

Reinhold Niebuhr

Love is not measured by what it gets, but by what it costs.

Oswald Chambers

How do you spell love? When you reach the point where the happiness, security, and development of another person is as much of a driving force to you as your own happiness, security, and development, then you have a mature love. True love is spelled G-I-V-E. It is not based on what you can get, but rooted in what you can give to the other person.

Josh McDowell

A PRAYER FOR TODAY

Dear Lord, You have given me the gift of love; let me share that gift with others. And, keep me mindful that the essence of love is not to receive it, but to give it, today and forever. Amen

CHAPTER 17

THE IMPORTANCE OF WORSHIP

*But an hour is coming, and is now here,
when the true worshipers will worship the Father
in spirit and truth. Yes, the Father wants
such people to worship Him. God is Spirit,
and those who worship Him must worship
in spirit and truth.*

—

JOHN 4:23-24 HCSB

All of mankind is engaged in worship of one kind or another. The question is not whether we worship, but what we worship. Some of us choose to worship God. The result is a plentiful harvest of joy, peace, and abundance. Others distance themselves from God by foolishly worshiping things of this earth such as fame, fortune, or personal gratification. To do so is a terrible mistake with eternal consequences.

Whenever we place our love for material possessions above our love for God—or when we yield to the countless temptations of this world—we find ourselves engaged in a struggle between good and evil, a clash between God and Satan. Our responses to these struggles have implications that echo throughout our families and throughout our communities.

How can we ensure that we cast our lot with God? We do so, in part, by the practice of regular, purposeful worship in the company of fellow believers. When we worship God faithfully and fervently, we are blessed. When we fail to worship God, for whatever reason, we forfeit the spiritual gifts that He intends for us.

We must worship our Heavenly Father, not just with our words, but also with deeds. We must honor Him, praise Him, and obey Him. As we seek to find purpose and meaning for our lives, we must first seek His purpose and His will. For believers, God comes first. Always first.

MORE PROMISES FROM GOD'S WORD

Worship the Lord your God and . . . serve Him only.

Matthew 4:10 HCSB

So that at the name of Jesus every knee should bow—of those who are in heaven and on earth and under the earth—and every tongue should confess that Jesus Christ is Lord, to the glory of God the Father.

Philippians 2:10-11 HCSB

If anyone is thirsty, he should come to Me and drink!

John 7:37 HCSB

MORE GREAT IDEAS

When God is at the center of your life, you worship. When he's not, you worry.

Rick Warren

Each time, before you intercede, be quiet first and worship God in His glory. Think of what He can do and how He delights to hear the prayers of His redeemed people. Think of your place and privilege in Christ, and expect great things!

Andrew Murray

I am of the opinion that we should not be concerned about working for God until we have learned the meaning and delight of worshipping Him.

A. W. Tozer

Inside the human heart is an undeniable, spiritual instinct to commune with its Creator.

Jim Cymbala

Worship is spiritual. Our worship must be more than just outward expression, it must also take place in our spirits.

Franklin Graham

Worship is a daunting task. Each worships differently. But each should worship.

Max Lucado

Worship is not taught from the pulpit. It must be learned in the heart.

Jim Elliot

Worship is your spirit responding to God's Spirit.

Rick Warren

A PRAYER FOR TODAY

Dear Lord, today I will worship You with my thoughts, my deeds, my words, and my prayers. Amen

CHAPTER 18

THE POWER OF PATIENCE

A patient spirit is better than a proud spirit.

—

ECCLESIASTES 7:8 HCSB

Are you a perfectly patient fellow? If so, feel free to skip the rest of this page. But if you're not, here's something to think about: If you really want to become a more patient person, God is ready and willing to help.

The Bible promises that when you sincerely seek God's help, He will give you the things that you need—and that includes patience. But God won't force you to become a more patient person. If you want to become a more mature Christian, you've got to do some of the work yourself—and the best time to start doing that work is now.

So, if you want to gain patience and maturity, bow your head and start praying about it. Then, rest assured that with God's help, you can most certainly make yourself a more patient, understanding, mature Christian.

MORE PROMISES FROM GOD'S WORD

Therefore the Lord is waiting to show you mercy, and is rising up to show you compassion, for the Lord is a just God. Happy are all who wait patiently for Him.

Isaiah 30:18 HCSB

Love is patient; love is kind.

1 Corinthians 13:4 HCSB

Be gentle to everyone, able to teach, and patient.

2 Timothy 2:23 HCSB

Now we exhort you, brethren, warn those who are unruly, comfort the fainthearted, uphold the weak, be patient with all.

1 Thessalonians 5:14 NKJV

My dearly loved brothers, understand this: everyone must be quick to hear, slow to speak, and slow to anger, for man's anger does not accomplish God's righteousness.

James 1:19-20 HCSB

MORE GREAT IDEAS

God is more patient with us than we are with ourselves.

Max Lucado

If God is diligent, surely we ought to be diligent in doing our duty to Him. Think how patient and diligent God has been to us!

Oswald Chambers

You can't step in front of God and not get in trouble. When He says, "Go three steps," don't go four.

Charles Stanley

In the Bible, patience is not a passive acceptance of circumstances. It is a courageous perseverance in the face of suffering and difficulty.

Warren Wiersbe

Our challenge is to wait in faith for the day of God's favor and salvation.

Jim Cymbala

In all negotiations of difficulties, a man may not look to sow and reap at once. He must prepare his business and so ripen it by degrees.

Francis Bacon

Grass that is here today and gone tomorrow does not require much time to mature. A big oak tree that lasts for generations requires much more time to grow and mature. God is concerned about your life through eternity. Allow Him to take all the time He needs to shape you for His purposes. Larger assignments will require longer periods of preparation.

Henry Blackaby

A PRAYER FOR TODAY

Dear Lord, give me wisdom and patience. When I am hurried, give me peace. When I am frustrated, give me perspective. When I am angry, keep me mindful of Your presence. Today, let me be a patient Christian, Lord, as I trust in You and in Your master plan for my life. Amen

CHAPTER 19

OBEY HIM

———

*Therefore, get your minds ready for action,
being self-disciplined, and set your hope
completely on the grace to be brought to you
at the revelation of Jesus Christ. As obedient
children, do not be conformed to the desires
of your former ignorance but, as the One
who called you is holy, you also are
to be holy in all your conduct.*

—

1 PETER 1:13-15 HCSB

We live in a world filled with temptations, distractions, and countless opportunities to disobey God. But as men who seek to be godly role models for our families, we must turn our thoughts and our hearts away from the evils of this world. We must turn instead to God.

Talking about God is easy; living by His commandments is considerably harder. But unless we are willing to abide by God's laws, our righteous proclamations ring hollow.

How can we best proclaim our love for the Lord? By obeying Him. We must seek God's counsel and trust the counsel He gives. And, when we invite God into our hearts and live according to His commandments, we are blessed today, and tomorrow, and forever.

MORE PROMISES FROM GOD'S WORD

Therefore, everyone who hears these words of Mine and acts on them will be like a sensible man who built his house on the rock. The rain fell, the rivers rose, and the winds blew and pounded that house. Yet it didn't collapse, because its foundation was on the rock.

Matthew 7:24–25 HCSB

I have sought You with all my heart; don't let me wander from Your commands.

Psalm 119:10 HCSB

Just then someone came up and asked Him, "Teacher, what good must I do to have eternal life?" "Why do you ask Me about what is good?" He said to him. "There is only One who is good. If you want to enter into life, keep the commandments."

Matthew 19:16-17 HCSB

Jesus answered, "If anyone loves Me, he will keep My word. My Father will love him, and We will come to him and make Our home with him."

John 14:23 HCSB

MORE GREAT IDEAS

Trials and sufferings teach us to obey the Lord by faith, and we soon learn that obedience pays off in joyful ways.

Bill Bright

When you suffer and lose, that does not mean you are being disobedient to God. In fact, it might mean you're right in the center of His will. The path of obedience is often marked by times of suffering and loss.

Charles Swindoll

Mary could not have dreamed all that would result from her faithful obedience. Likewise, you cannot possibly imagine all that God has in store for you when you trust him.

Henry Blackaby

Only he who believes is obedient. Only he who is obedient believes.

Dietrich Bonhoeffer

You can't step in front of God and not get in trouble. When He says, "Go three steps," don't go four.

Charles Stanley

Obedience is the road to freedom, humility the road to pleasure, unity the road to personality.

C. S. Lewis

True faith commits us to obedience.

A. W. Tozer

A PRAYER FOR TODAY

Dear Heavenly Father, You have blessed me with a love that is infinite and eternal. Let me demonstrate my love for You by obeying Your commandments. Make me a faithful servant, Father, today and throughout eternity. And, let me show my love for You by sharing Your message and Your love with others. Amen

CHAPTER 20

THE IMPORTANCE OF DISCIPLINE

—※◦❊◦※—

No discipline seems enjoyable at the time,
but painful. Later on, however,
it yields the fruit of peace and righteousness to
those who have been trained by it.

—

HEBREWS 12:11 HCSB

The words disciple and discipline are both derived from Latin, so it's not surprising that when you become a disciple of Christ you should expect to exercise self-discipline in all matters. Self-discipline is not simply a proven way to get ahead; it's also an integral part of God's plan for your life. So if you genuinely seek to be a faithful steward of your time, your talents, and your resources, you must adopt a disciplined approach to life. Otherwise, your talents are likely to go unused, and your resources are likely to be squandered.

Most of life's greatest rewards come as the result of hard work and perseverance. May you, as a disciplined disciple, be willing to do the work—and keep doing it—until you've earned the rewards that God has in store for you.

MORE PROMISES FROM GOD'S WORD

For this very reason, make every effort to supplement your faith with goodness, goodness with knowledge, knowledge with self-control, self-control with endurance, endurance with godliness.

2 Peter 1:5-6 HCSB

The one who follows instruction is on the path to life, but the one who rejects correction goes astray.

Proverbs 10:17 HCSB

I discipline my body and bring it under strict control, so that after preaching to others, I myself will not be disqualified.

1 Corinthians 9:27 HCSB

Therefore by their fruits you will know them.

Matthew 7:20 NKJV

But each person should examine his own work, and then he will have a reason for boasting in himself alone, and not in respect to someone else. For each person will have to carry his own load.

Galatians 6:4-5 HCSB

MORE GREAT IDEAS

Discipline is training that develops and corrects.

Charles Stanley

Work is doing it. Discipline is doing it every day. Diligence is doing it well every day.

Dave Ramsey

The Bible calls for discipline and a recognition of authority. Children must learn this at home.

Billy Graham

Personal humility is a spiritual discipline and the hallmark of the service of Jesus.

Franklin Graham

As we seek to become disciples of Jesus Christ, we should never forget that the word disciple is directly related to the word discipline. To be a disciple of the Lord Jesus Christ is to know his discipline.

Dennis Swanberg

God cannot build character without our cooperation. If we resist Him, then He chastens us into submission. But, if we submit to Him, then He can accomplish His work. He is not satisfied with a halfway job. God wants a perfect work; He wants a finished product that is mature and complete.

Warren Wiersbe

If one examines the secret behind a championship football team, a magnificent orchestra, or a successful business, the principal ingredient is invariably discipline.

James Dobson

A PRAYER FOR TODAY

Dear Lord, I want to be a disciplined believer. Let me use my time wisely, let me obey Your commandments faithfully, and let me worship You joyfully, today and every day. Amen

CHAPTER 21

LIFETIME LEARNING

Now if any of you lacks wisdom, he should ask God, who gives to all generously and without criticizing, and it will be given to him.

—

JAMES 1:5 HCSB

Whether you're twenty-two or a hundred and two, you've still got lots to learn. Even if you're very wise, God isn't finished with you yet, and He isn't finished teaching you important lessons about life here on earth and life eternal.

God does not intend for you to be a stagnant believer. Far from it! God wants you to continue growing as a person and as a Christian every day that you live. And make no mistake: both spiritual and intellectual growth are possible during every stage of life.

Are you a curious Christian who has committed yourself to the regimen of regular Bible study, or do you consult your Bible on a hit-or-miss basis? The answer to this question will be an indication of the extent to which you allow God to direct the course of your life.

As a spiritual being, you have the potential to grow in your personal knowledge of the Lord every day that you live. You can do so through prayer, through worship, through an openness to God's Holy Spirit, and through a careful study of God's Holy Word. Your Bible contains powerful prescriptions for everyday living. If you sincerely seek to walk with God, you should commit yourself to the thoughtful study of His teachings.

Do you seek to live a life of righteousness and wisdom? If so, you must continue to study the ultimate source of wisdom: the Word of God. You must associate, day in and day out, with godly men and women. And, you must act in accordance with your beliefs.

When you study God's Word and live according to His commandments, you will become wise . . . and you will serve as a shining example to your friends, to your family, and to the world.

MORE PROMISES FROM GOD'S WORD

Buy—and do not sell—truth, wisdom, instruction, and understanding.

Proverbs 23:23 HCSB

For now we see indistinctly, as in a mirror, but then face to face. Now I know in part, but then I will know fully, as I am fully known.

1 Corinthians 13:12 HCSB

MORE GREAT IDEAS

God's plan for our guidance is for us to grow gradually in wisdom before we get to the crossroads.

Bill Hybels

Wise people listen to wise instruction, especially instruction from the Word of God.

Warren Wiersbe

Kids aren't looking for perfect parents, but they are looking for honest and growing ones.

Howard Hendricks

Don't expect wisdom to come into your life like great chunks of rock on a conveyor belt. Wisdom comes privately from God as a by-product of right decisions, godly reactions, and the application of spiritual principles to daily circumstances.

Charles Swindoll

It's the things you learn after you know it all that really count.

Vance Havner

The wise man gives proper appreciation in his life to his past. He learns to sift the sawdust of heritage in order to find the nuggets that make the current moment have any meaning.

Grady Nutt

The vigor of our spiritual lives will be in exact proportion to the place held by the Bible in our lives and in our thoughts.

George Mueller

A PRAYER FOR TODAY

Dear Lord, I have so much to learn. Help me to watch, to listen, to think, and to learn, every day of my life. Amen

CHAPTER 22

FORGIVENESS NOW

———❖———

*All bitterness, anger and wrath, insult and
slander must be removed from you, along with
all wickedness. And be kind and compassionate
to one another, forgiving one another,
just as God also forgave you in Christ.*

—

EPHESIANS 4:31-32 HCSB

Are you the kind of man who carries a grudge? If so, you know sometimes it's very tough to forgive the people who have hurt you. And that's too bad because life would be much simpler if we could forgive people "once and for all" and be done with it. But forgiveness is seldom that easy. For most of us, the decision to forgive is straightforward, but the process of forgiving is more difficult. Forgiveness is a journey that requires effort, time, perseverance, and prayer.

Forgiveness is seldom easy, but it is always right. When we forgive those who have hurt us, we honor God by obeying His commandments. But when we harbor bitterness against others, we disobey God—with predictably unhappy results.

If there exists even one person whom you have not forgiven (including yourself), follow God's commandment and His will for your life: forgive that person today. And remember that bitterness, anger, and regret are not part of God's plan for your life. Forgiveness is.

If you sincerely wish to forgive someone, pray for that person. And then pray for yourself by asking God to heal your heart. Don't expect forgiveness to be easy or quick, but rest assured: with God as your partner, you can forgive . . . and you will.

MORE PROMISES FROM GOD'S WORD

A person's insight gives him patience, and his virtue is to overlook an offense.

Proverbs 19:11 HCSB

See to it that no one repays evil for evil to anyone, but always pursue what is good for one another and for all.

1 Thessalonians 5:15 HCSB

And forgive us our sins, for we ourselves also forgive everyone in debt to us.

Luke 11:4 HCSB

Be merciful, just as your Father also is merciful.

Luke 6:36 HCSB

MORE GREAT IDEAS

By not forgiving, by not letting wrongs go, we aren't getting back at anyone. We are merely punishing ourselves by barricading our own hearts.

Jim Cymbala

To hold on to hate and resentments is to throw a monkey wrench into the machinery of life.

E. Stanley Jones

Give me such love for God and men as will blot out all hatred and bitterness.

Dietrich Bonhoeffer

God forgets the past. Imitate him.

Max Lucado

Our forgiveness toward others should flow from a realization and appreciation of God's forgiveness toward us.

Franklin Graham

Forgiveness is God's command.

Martin Luther

The love of God is revealed in that He laid down His life for His enemies.

Oswald Chambers

Miracles broke the physical laws of the universe; forgiveness broke the moral rules.

Philip Yancey

A PRAYER FOR TODAY

Heavenly Father, give me a forgiving heart. When I am bitter, Your Word reminds me that forgiveness is Your commandment. Let me be Your obedient servant, Lord, and let me be a man who forgives others just as You have forgiven me. Amen

CHAPTER 23

BEING A FAITHFUL STEWARD

Let a man so consider us, as servants of Christ
and stewards of the mysteries of God.
Moreover it is required in stewards
that one be found faithful.

—

1 CORINTHIANS 4:1-2 NKJV

Do you seek to be a righteous follower of Christ? Do you earnestly seek God's will for your life? And do you trust God's promises? If so, then you will be a faithful steward of the gifts He has given you.

Oswald Chambers advised, "Never support an experience which does not have God as its source, and faith in God as its result." And so it is with our tithes. When we return to God that which is rightfully His, we experience the spiritual growth that always accompanies obedience to Him. But, when we attempt to shortchange our Creator, either materially or spiritually, we distance ourselves from God. The consequences of our disobedience are as predictable as they are tragic.

As Christians, we are called to walk with God and to obey His commandments. To do so is an act of holiness. God deserves our obedience. May we obey Him in all things, including our tithes.

MORE PROMISES FROM GOD'S WORD

Well done, good and faithful servant; you were faithful over a few things, I will make you ruler over many things. Enter into the joy of your lord.

Matthew 25:21 NKJV

Based on the gift they have received, everyone should use it to serve others, as good managers of the varied grace of God.

1 Peter 4:10 HCSB

He that giveth, let him do it with simplicity....

Romans 12:8 KJV

For I am the Lord, I do not change. . . . Will a man rob God? Yet you have robbed Me! But you say, in what way have we robbed You? In tithes and offerings. You are cursed with a curse, for you have robbed Me, even this whole nation. Bring all the tithes into the storehouse, that there may be food in My house.

Malachi 3:6, 8-10 NKJV

MORE GREAT IDEAS

We are never more like God than when we give.

Charles Swindoll

Christians have become victims of one of the most devious plots Satan ever created—the concept that money belongs to us and not to God.

Larry Burkett

A steward does not own, but instead manages, all that his master puts into his hands.

Warren Wiersbe

If our charities do not at all pinch or hamper us, I should say they are too small. There ought to be things we should like to do and cannot do because our charitable expenditure excludes them.

C. S. Lewis

God will withdraw resources from the poor stewards, as related in Matthew 25, and give it to the good stewards.

Bill Bright

A steward is one who manages another's resources. Each of us is a manager, not an owner. God is the owner, and we are to manage according to His plan.

Larry Burkett

A PRAYER FOR TODAY

Dear Lord, make me a faithful steward of my possessions, my talents, my time, and my testimony. In every aspect of my life, Father, let me be Your humble, obedient servant. I trust, Father, that You will provide for me now and throughout eternity. And I will obey Your commandment that I give sacrificially to the needs of Your Church. Amen

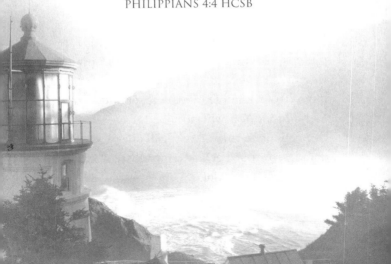

CHAPTER 24

REJOICE ALWAYS

Rejoice in the Lord always.
I will say it again: Rejoice!

—

PHILIPPIANS 4:4 HCSB

God's Word makes it clear: He intends that His joy should become our joy. The Lord intends that believers should share His love with His joy in their hearts. Yet sometimes, amid the inevitable hustle and bustle of life here on earth, we can forfeit—albeit temporarily—God's joy as we wrestle with the challenges of daily living.

Psalm 100 reminds us that, as believers, we have every reason to celebrate: "Shout for joy to the LORD, all the earth. Worship the LORD with gladness" (vv. 1-2 NIV). These words most certainly apply to you.

Are you a man whose joy is clearly evident to your family and friends? If so, congratulations—you're doing God's will. But, if you find yourself feeling discouraged or worse, it's time to slow down and have a quiet conversation with your Creator.

If your heart is heavy, turn to Christ. He will give you peace and joy. And if you already have the joy of Christ in your heart, share it freely, just as Christ has freely shared His joy with you.

MORE PROMISES FROM GOD'S WORD

Now I am coming to You, and I speak these things in the world so that they may have My joy completed in them.

John 17:13 HCSB

Make me to hear joy and gladness.

Psalm 51:8 KJV

So you also have sorrow now. But I will see you again. Your hearts will rejoice, and no one will rob you of your joy.

John 16:22 HCSB

Weeping may spend the night, but there is joy in the morning.

Psalm 30:5 HCSB

Glory in His holy name; let the hearts of those rejoice who seek the Lord! Seek the Lord and His strength; seek His face evermore!

1 Chronicles 16:10-11 NKJV

MORE GREAT IDEAS

Gratitude changes the pangs of memory into a tranquil joy.

Dietrich Bonhoeffer

Joy is the direct result of having God's perspective on our daily lives and the effect of loving our Lord enough to obey His commands and trust His promises.

Bill Bright

We all sin by needlessly disobeying the apostolic injunction to rejoice.

C. S. Lewis

The ability to rejoice in any situation is a sign of spiritual maturity.

Billy Graham

A life of intimacy with God is characterized by joy.

Oswald Chambers

Today you will encounter God's creation. When you see the beauty around you, let each detail remind you to lift your head in praise.

Max Lucado

Joy is the heart's harmonious response to the Lord's song of love.

A. W. Tozer

Rejoice, the Lord is King; Your Lord and King adore! Rejoice, give thanks and sing and triumph evermore.

Charles Wesley

A PRAYER FOR TODAY

Dear Lord, You are my loving Heavenly Father, and You created me in Your image. As Your faithful child, I will make Your joy my joy. I will praise Your works, I will obey Your Word, and I will honor Your Son, this day and every day of my life. Amen

CHAPTER 25

PRAISE HIM EVERY DAY

—◦—

Praise the Lord, all nations! Glorify Him,
all peoples! For great is His faithful love to us;
the Lord's faithfulness endures forever.
Hallelujah!

—

PSALM 117 HCSB

When is the best time to praise God? In church? Before dinner is served? When we tuck little children into bed? None of the above. The best time to praise God is all day, every day, to the greatest extent we can, with thanksgiving in our hearts.

Too many of us, even well-intentioned believers, tend to "compartmentalize" our waking hours into a few familiar categories: work, rest, play, family time, and worship. To do so is a mistake. Worship and praise should be woven into the fabric of everything we do; it should never be relegated to a weekly three-hour visit to church on Sunday morning.

Mrs. Charles E. Cowman, the author of the classic devotional text, *Streams in the Desert*, wrote, "Two wings are necessary to lift our souls toward God: prayer and praise. Prayer asks. Praise accepts the answer." Today, find a little more time to lift your concerns to God in prayer, and praise Him for all that He has done. He's listening . . . and He wants to hear from you.

MORE PROMISES FROM GOD'S WORD

Therefore, through Him let us continually offer up to God a sacrifice of praise, that is, the fruit of our lips that confess His name.

Hebrews 13:15 HCSB

But I will hope continually and will praise You more and more.

Psalm 71:14 HCSB

So that at the name of Jesus every knee should bow—of those who are in heaven and on earth and under the earth—and every tongue should confess that Jesus Christ is Lord, to the glory of God the Father.

Philippians 2:10-11 HCSB

Enter into his gates with thanksgiving, and into his courts with praise: be thankful unto him, and bless his name. For the LORD is good; his mercy is everlasting; and his truth endureth to all generations.

Psalm 100:4-5 KJV

MORE GREAT IDEAS

Praise is the highest occupation of any being.

Max Lucado

Why wait until the fourth Thursday in November? Why wait until the morning of December twenty-fifth? Thanksgiving to God should be an everyday affair. The time to be thankful is now!

Jim Gallery

The words "thank" and "think" come from the same root word. If we would think more, we would thank more.

Warren Wiersbe

A child of God should be a visible beatitude for joy and a living doxology for gratitude.

C. H. Spurgeon

It is only with gratitude that life becomes rich.

Dietrich Bonhoeffer

Praise reestablishes the proper chain of command; we recognize that the King is on the throne and that he has saved his people.

Max Lucado

Thank God every morning when you get up that you have something to do that day which must be done, whether you like it or not.

Charles Kingsley

Holy, holy, holy! Lord God Almighty! All Thy works shall praise Thy name in earth, and sky, and sea.

Reginald Heber

A PRAYER FOR TODAY

Dear Lord, make me a man who gives constant praise to You. And, let me share the joyous news of Jesus Christ with a world that needs His transformation and His salvation. Amen

CHAPTER 26

SEARCHING FOR TRUTH

—∗◦∗—

For everyone who practices wicked things hates the light and avoids it, so that his deeds may not be exposed. But anyone who lives by the truth comes to the light, so that his works may be shown to be accomplished by God.

—

JOHN 3:20–21 HCSB

Would you like a rock-solid, time-tested formula for success? Here it is: Seek God's truth, and live by it. Of course this strategy may sound simple, and it may sound somewhat old-fashioned, especially if you're a fast-track, dues-paying citizen of the 21st century. But God's truth never goes out of style. And God's wisdom is as valid today as it was when He laid the foundations of the universe.

The familiar words of John 8:32 remind us that "you shall know the truth, and the truth shall make you free" (NKJV). And St. Augustine had this advice: "Let everything perish! Dismiss these empty vanities! And let us take up the search for the truth."

God is vitally concerned with truth. His Word teaches the truth; His Spirit reveals the truth; His Son leads us to the truth. When we open our hearts to God, and when we allow His Son to rule over our thoughts and our lives, God reveals Himself, and we come to understand the truth about ourselves and the Truth about God's gift of grace.

Are you seeking God's truth and making decisions in light of that truth? Hopefully so.

When you do, you'll discover that the truth will indeed set you free, now and forever.

MORE PROMISES FROM GOD'S WORD

I have no greater joy than this: to hear that my children are walking in the truth.

3 John 1:4 HCSB

Be diligent to present yourself approved to God, a worker who doesn't need to be ashamed, correctly teaching the word of truth.

2 Timothy 2:15 HCSB

You have already heard about this hope in the message of truth, the gospel that has come to you. It is bearing fruit and growing all over the world, just as it has among you since the day you heard it and recognized God's grace in the truth.

Colossians 1:5-6 HCSB

When the Spirit of truth comes, He will guide you into all the truth.

John 16:13 HCSB

MORE GREAT IDEAS

Having a doctrine pass before the mind is not what the Bible means by knowing the truth. It's only when it reaches down deep into the heart that the truth begins to set us free, just as a key must penetrate a lock to turn it, or as rainfall must saturate the earth down to the roots in order for your garden to grow.

John Eldredge

Lying covers a multitude of sins—temporarily.

D. L. Moody

You cannot glorify Christ and practice deception at the same time.

Warren Wiersbe

Honesty has a beautiful and refreshing simplicity about it. No ulterior motives. No hidden meanings. As honesty and integrity characterize our lives, there will be no need to manipulate others.

Charles Swindoll

For Christians, God himself is the only absolute; truth and ethics are rooted in his character.

Chuck Colson

The only people who achieve much are those who want knowledge so badly that they seek it while the conditions are still unfavorable. Favorable conditions never come.

C. S. Lewis

We have in Jesus Christ a perfect example of how to put God's truth into practice.

Bill Bright

A PRAYER FOR TODAY

Dear Lord, Jesus said He was the truth, and I believe Him. Father, may Jesus always be the standard for truth in my life so that I might be a worthy example to others and a worthy servant to You. Amen

CHAPTER 27

COUNTING YOUR BLESSINGS

You will show me the path of life;
in Your presence is fullness of joy;
at Your right hand are pleasures forevermore.

—

PSALM 16:11 NKJV

I f you sat down and began counting your blessings, how long would it take? A very, very long time! Your blessings include life, freedom, family, friends, talents, and possessions, for starters. But, your greatest blessing—a gift that is yours for the asking—is God's gift of salvation through Christ Jesus.

Are you a thankful believer who takes time each day to take a partial inventory of the gifts God has given you? Hopefully you are that kind of Christian. After all, God's Word makes it clear: a wise heart is a thankful heart.

We honor God, in part, by the genuine gratitude we feel in our hearts for the blessings He has bestowed upon us. Yet even the most saintly among us must endure periods of fear, doubt, and regret. Why? Because we are imperfect human beings who are incapable of perfect gratitude. Still, even on life's darker days, we must seek to cleanse our hearts of negative emotions and fill them, instead, with praise, with love, with hope, and with thanksgiving. To do otherwise is to be unfair to ourselves, to our loved ones, and to our God.

Sometimes, life can be complicated, demanding, and frustrating. When the demands of life leave us rushing from place to place with scarcely a moment to spare, we may fail to pause and thank our Creator for His gifts. But, whenever we neglect to give proper thanks to the Father, we suffer because of our misplaced priorities.

Today, begin making a list of your blessings. You most certainly will not be able to make a complete list, but take a few moments and jot down as many blessings as you can. Then, give thanks to the Giver of all good things: God. His love for you is eternal, as are His gifts. And it's never too soon—or too late—to offer Him thanks.

Come to terms with God and be at peace; in this way good will come to you.

Job 22:21 HCSB

MORE PROMISES FROM GOD'S WORD

I will make them and the area around My hill a blessing: I will send down showers in their season— showers of blessing.

Ezekiel 34:26 HCSB

Blessed is a man who endures trials, because when he passes the test he will receive the crown of life that He has promised to those who love Him.

James 1:12 HCSB

The Lord bless you and keep you; the Lord make His face shine upon you, and be gracious to you.

Numbers 6:24-25 NKJV

I will make you a great nation; I will bless you and make your name great; and you shall be a blessing. I will bless those who bless you, and I will curse him who curses you; and in you all the families of the earth shall be blessed.

Genesis 12:2-3 NKJV

MORE GREAT IDEAS

God's love for His children is unconditional, no strings attached. But, God's blessings on our lives do come with a condition—obedience. If we are to receive the fullness of God's blessings, we must obey Him and keep His commandments.

Jim Gallery

With the goodness of God to desire our highest welfare and the wisdom of God to plan it, what do we lack? Surely we are the most favored of all creatures.

A. W. Tozer

Grace is an outrageous blessing bestowed freely on a totally undeserving recipient.

Bill Hybels

The Christian life is motivated, not by a list of do's and don'ts, but by the gracious outpouring of God's love and blessing.

Anne Graham Lotz

It is when we give ourselves to be a blessing that we can specially count on the blessing of God.

Andrew Murray

Blessings can either humble us and draw us closer to God or allow us to become full of pride and self-sufficiency.

Jim Cymbala

God blesses us in spite of our lives and not because of our lives.

Max Lucado

A PRAYER FOR TODAY

Lord, You have given me so much, and I am thankful. Today, I seek Your blessings for my life, and I know that every good thing You give me is to be shared with others. I am blessed that I might be a blessing to those around me, Father. Let me give thanks for Your gifts . . . and let me share them. Amen

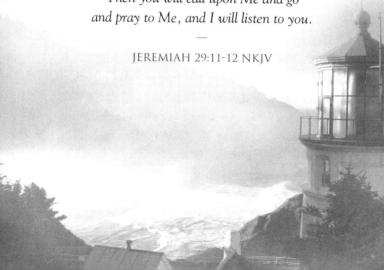

CHAPTER 28

BE HOPEFUL

For I know the thoughts that I think toward you,
says the Lord, thoughts of peace and not of evil,
to give you a future and a hope.
Then you will call upon Me and go
and pray to Me, and I will listen to you.

—

JEREMIAH 29:11-12 NKJV

Look around you. Read the newspaper. Watch the evening news. When you think about the things that are going on in Washington or elsewhere in the world, it's possible to lose hope. But God provides an antidote to despair. One of the rewards of spending time before the face of God is the gift of divine hope.

Have you ever felt your hope in the future slipping away? If so, here's what you should do: study God's Word, seek God's will, and spend prayerful hours before God's face. When you do, you'll discover the hope that is the possession of those who place their trust in Him.

This world can be a place of trials and tribulations, but as believers in Christ we are secure. We need never lose hope because God has promised us peace, joy, and eternal life. So, let us face each day with hope in our hearts and trust in our God. And, let us teach our children to do likewise. After all, God has promised us that we are His throughout eternity, and He keeps His promises. Always.

MORE PROMISES FROM GOD'S WORD

Now may the God of hope fill you with all joy and peace in believing, so that you may overflow with hope by the power of the Holy Spirit.

Romans 15:13 HCSB

But if we hope for what we do not see, we eagerly wait for it with patience.

Romans 8:25 HCSB

Rejoice in hope; be patient in affliction; be persistent in prayer.

Romans 12:12 HCSB

Lord, I turn my hope to You. My God, I trust in You. Do not let me be disgraced; do not let my enemies gloat over me.

Psalm 25:1-2 HCSB

Let us hold on to the confession of our hope without wavering, for He who promised is faithful.

Hebrews 10:23 HCSB

MORE GREAT IDEAS

People are genuinely motivated by hope and a part of that hope is the assurance of future glory with God for those who are His people.

Warren Wiersbe

I wish I could make it all new again; I can't. But God can. "He restores my soul," wrote the shepherd. God doesn't reform; he restores. He doesn't camouflage the old; he restores the new. The Master Builder will pull out the original plan and restore it. He will restore the vigor, he will restore the energy. He will restore the hope. He will restore the soul.

Max Lucado

Our hope in Christ for the future is the mainstream of our joy.

C. H. Spurgeon

Faith looks back and draws courage; hope looks ahead and keeps desire alive.

John Eldredge

The hope we have in Jesus is the anchor for the soul—something sure and steadfast, preventing drifting or giving way, lowered to the depth of God's love.

Franklin Graham

Hope is nothing more than the expectation of those things which faith has believed to be truly promised by God.

John Calvin

A PRAYER FOR TODAY

Dear Lord, make me a man of hope. If I become discouraged, let me turn to You. If I grow weary, let me seek strength in You. When I face adversity, let me seek Your will and trust Your Word. In every aspect of my life, I will trust You, Father, so that my heart will be filled with faith and hope, this day and forever. Amen

CHAPTER 29

FINDING PEACE

———⊰⊱———

The peace of God, which surpasses
all understanding, will guard your hearts
and minds through Christ Jesus.

—

PHILIPPIANS 4:7 NKJV

Our world is in a state of constant change and so are we. God is not. At times, everything around us seems to be changing: our children are growing up, we are growing older, loved ones pass on. Sometimes, the world seems to be trembling beneath our feet. But we can be comforted in the knowledge that our Heavenly Father is the rock that cannot be shaken.

Are you at peace with the direction of your life? If you're a Christian, you should be. Perhaps you seek a new direction or a sense of renewed purpose, but those feelings should never rob you of the genuine peace that can and should be yours through a personal relationship with Jesus. The demands of everyday living should never obscure the fact that Christ died so that you might have life abundant and eternal.

Have you found the lasting peace that can be yours through Jesus, or are you still rushing after the illusion of "peace and happiness" that our world promises but cannot deliver? The world's "peace" is fleeting; Christ's peace is forever.

Christ is standing at the door, waiting patiently for you to invite Him to reign in your heart. His eternal peace is offered freely. Claim it today.

MORE PROMISES FROM GOD'S WORD

Abundant peace belongs to those who love Your instruction; nothing makes them stumble.

Psalm 119:165 HCSB

If possible, on your part, live at peace with everyone.

Romans 12:18 HCSB

Blessed are the peacemakers, for they shall be called sons of God.

Matthew 5:9 NKJV

And suddenly there was with the angel a multitude of the heavenly host praising God and saying: "Glory to God in the highest, and on earth peace, goodwill toward men!"

Luke 2:13-14 NKJV

MORE GREAT IDEAS

That peace, which has been described and which believers enjoy, is a participation of the peace which their glorious Lord and Master himself enjoys.

Jonathan Edwards

Peace is the deepest thing a human personality can know; it is almighty.

Oswald Chambers

We're prone to want God to change our circumstances, but He wants to change our character. We think that peace comes from the outside in, but it comes from the inside out.

Warren Wiersbe

A great many people are trying to make peace, but that has already been done. God has not left it for us to do; all we have to do is to enter into it.

D. L. Moody

Thou hast formed us for Thyself, and our hearts are restless till they find rest in Thee.

St. Augustine

What peace can they have who are not at peace with God?

Matthew Henry

He keeps us in perfect peace while He whispers His secrets and reveals His counsels.

Oswald Chambers

Peace with God is where all peace begins.

Jim Gallery

A PRAYER FOR TODAY

Dear Lord, You give me peace. I thank You, Father, for Your love, for Your peace, and for Your Son. Amen

CHAPTER 30

FOR GOD SO LOVED THE WORLD

———◆———

For God so loved the world, that he gave his only begotten Son, that whosoever believeth in him should not perish, but have everlasting life.

—

JOHN 3:16 KJV

God's grace is not earned . . . thank goodness! To earn God's love and His gift of eternal life would be far beyond the abilities of even the most righteous man or woman. Thankfully, grace is not an earthly reward for righteous behavior; it is a blessed spiritual gift which can be accepted by believers who dedicate themselves to God through Christ. When we accept Christ into our hearts, we are saved by His grace.

The familiar words of Ephesians 2:8 make God's promise perfectly clear: It is by grace we have been saved, through faith. We are saved not because of our good deeds but because of our faith in Christ.

God's grace is the ultimate gift, and we owe to Him the ultimate in thanksgiving. Let us praise the Creator for His priceless gift, and let us share the Good News with all who cross our paths. We return our Father's love by accepting His grace and by sharing His message and His love.

Have you thanked God today for blessings that are too numerous to count? Have you offered Him your heartfelt prayers and your wholehearted praise? If not, it's time slow down and offer a prayer of thanksgiving to the One who has given you life on earth and life eternal.

If you are a thoughtful Christian, you will be a thankful Christian. No matter your circumstances, you owe God so much more than you can ever repay, and you owe Him your heartfelt thanks. So thank Him . . . and keep thanking Him, today, tomorrow and forever.

You, therefore, my child, be strong in the grace that is in Christ Jesus.

—

2 Timothy 2:1 HCSB

MORE PROMISES FROM GOD'S WORD

Therefore let us approach the throne of grace with boldness, so that we may receive mercy and find grace to help us at the proper time.

Hebrews 4:16 HCSB

For the law was given through Moses; grace and truth came through Jesus Christ.

John 1:17 HCSB

Therefore, since we are receiving a kingdom that cannot be shaken, let us hold on to grace. By it, we may serve God acceptably, with reverence and awe.

Hebrews 12:28 HCSB

But God, who is abundant in mercy, because of His great love that He had for us, made us alive with the Messiah even though we were dead in trespasses. By grace you are saved!

Ephesians 2:4-5 HCSB

MORE GREAT IDEAS

When I consider my existence beyond the grace, I am filled with confidence and gratitude because God has made an inviolable commitment to take me to heaven on the merits of Christ.

Bill Hybels

When you experience grace and are loved when you do not deserve it, you spend the rest of your life standing on tiptoes trying to reach His plan for your life out of gratitude.

Charles Stanley

While grace cannot grow more, we can grow more in it.

C. H. Spurgeon

Once grace has scrubbed the soul, anyone can take their place in the lineage of the Son of God.

Calvin Miller

If we only believe and ask, a full measure of God's grace is available to any of us.

Charles Swindoll

God shares Himself generously and graciously.

Eugene Peterson

No one is beyond His grace. No situation, anywhere on earth, is too hard for God.

Jim Cymbala

A PRAYER FOR TODAY

Accepting Your grace can be hard, Lord. Somehow, I feel that I must earn Your love and Your acceptance. Yet, the Bible promises that You love me and save me by Your grace. It is a gift I can only accept and cannot earn. Thank You for Your priceless, everlasting gift. Amen